POWER SNACKS

POWER SNACKS

50 SUPER HEALTHY SNACKS

PACKED WITH NUTRIENTS

LOVE FOOD™

This edition published by Parragon Books Ltd in 2015 and distributed by

Parragon Inc.
440 Park Avenue South, 13th Floor
New York, NY 10016
www.parragon.com/lovefood

LOVE FOOD is an imprint of Parragon Books Ltd

ISBN 978-1-4723-7596-4

Printed in China

Project managed by Andrea O'Connor
Designed by Persephone Coelho
New recipes by Sara Lewis
New photography by Ian Garlick
Edited by Fiona Biggs

Notes for the Reader

This book uses standard kitchen measuring spoons and cups. All spoon and cup measurements are level unless otherwise indicated. Unless otherwise stated, milk is assumed to be whole, eggs are large, individual vegetables are medium, and pepper is freshly ground black pepper. Unless otherwise stated, all root vegetables should be peeled prior to using.

Garnishes, decorations, and serving suggestions are all optional and not necessarily included in the recipe ingredients or method. Any optional ingredients and seasoning to taste are not included in the nutritional analysis. The times given are only an approximate guide. Preparation times differ according to the techniques used by different people and the cooking times may also vary from those given. Optional ingredients, variations, or serving suggestions have not been included in the time calculations.

While the author has made all reasonable efforts to ensure that the information contained in this book is accurate and up to date at the time of publication, anyone reading this book should note the following important points:

Medical and pharmaceutical knowledge is constantly changing and the author and the publisher cannot and do not guarantee the accuracy or appropriateness of the contents of this book;

In any event, this book is not intended to be, and should not be relied upon, as a substitute for appropriate, tailored professional advice. Both the author and the publisher strongly recommend that a physician or other healthcare professional is consulted before embarking on major dietary changes;

For the reasons set out above, and to the fullest extent permitted by law, the author and publisher: (i) cannot and do not accept any legal duty of care or responsibility in relation to the accuracy or appropriateness of the contents of this book, even where expressed as "advice" or using other words to this effect; and (ii) disclaim any liability, loss, damage, or risk that may be claimed or incurred as a consequence—directly or indirectly—of the use and/or application of any of the contents of this book.

CONTENTS

INTRODUCTION

Do you often find yourself feeling like you're "running on empty" in the middle of the afternoon, desperate for a snack to help you keep going? While a slice of cake or chocolate candy bar might seem like an obvious choice for a quick boost, they will soon make your energy levels plummet and can leave you feeling even more exhausted than before.

To fuel our bodies effectively—without the roller coaster of highs and lows—we need good-quality protein, healthy fats, some carbohydrates, and plenty of vegetables. Choosing snacks that are nutrient-dense, rich in superfoods, and made with smart, complex carbs will mean you are able to stay full for longer. Whole grains, nuts, seeds, meat, fruit, and vegetables all form a good foundation for healthy snacks, and you don't even need to give up the chocolate completely—just be sure to choose dark chocolate, preferably with a minimum of 70 percent cocoa solids, instead of sugar-laden milk chocolate.

Obesity levels are steadily rising and the main culprit is the amount of sugar and processed ingredients in our diet. While we might all love a drive-through snack of hamburger and fries or a sugary donut, they are full of empty calories, saturated fats, and highly processed sugars and salt, all of which offer little to no nutritional value.

Have you ever looked at the ingredients list on the packaging of your favorite store-bought snack? In addition to the main ingredient, a host of sweeteners, flavorings, and additives often follow, with ingredients you have probably never heard of included to prolong the shelf life. These chemical bad boys are quickly forgotten when we're reaching for a cookie at 3:30 p.m., but you can avoid them completely by preparing your own nutritious and sustainable power snacks.

Made with simple, readily available ingredients, homemade power snacks can be prepared with minimal fuss and expense. Source raw ingredients from your local farmers' market, supermarket, and health-food store to create delicious snacks packed with essential vitamins, minerals, protein, and good fats.

Complex carbs are great for filling a hole between meals—they take longer for the body to digest and help stabilize blood sugar to keep you on an even keel throughout the day without the crashes and cravings.

Choose from rolled oats, popcorn, quinoa, whole-grain rice, sweet potato, or pumpkin. The other essential ingredient in feeling full is protein, but you don't need to eat a large steak to get it. Nuts and seeds are great protein sources, too, and are easy to transport and graze on when out and about.

When it comes to fat, it's important to make the distinction between the harmful trans fats found in fried, fast, and processed food and natural and intensely healthy fats. Not only are these good for you, but you cannot survive without them, because they contain essential fatty acids that aid the absorption of important fat-soluble vitamins, such as A, D, E, and K. These fats can be found in certain ingredients, such as whole milk and cheese, butter, oily fish, olive oil, and nuts and seeds. They might register high on a calorie count, but they are healthy fats and this is the important part. Focusing more on the nutritional profile of foods instead of their caloric status allows us to eat the whole and natural ingredients our bodies need for optimum health.

We should all be eating a minimum of five portions of fruit and vegetables a day, but some statistics suggest that not enough of us are reaching this target. Sneaking them into snacks is a great way to be sure you're getting the recommended amount of these essential foods. And you don't need to rely on a simple apple or carrot stick to meet your quota—by using fruit and vegetables as the foundation of your power snacks, you can make sure you get a good dose throughout the day.

In this book, you will find a wide range of fresh, natural, and superhealthy snacks to choose from. An "On the Go" chapter contains delicious snacks to carry with you while you're out and about, meaning you'll be less tempted by fast-food alternatives. A whole chapter on "Take to Work" snacks has the office covered as well, with a variety of sweet and not-so-sweet bites to have on hand when the 3:30 p.m. sugar dip hits. "High Energy" includes high-protein, energy-spiking suggestions for snacks, ideal for pre- and post-workouts. Designed for days when you have a little more time to prepare, the "Weekend Snacks" chapter includes mouth-watering snacks to be enjoyed at leisure, while the "Sweet Indulgence" chapter offers a go-to collection of recipes for any sugary taste or craving.

Designed to change the way you snack and fuel your body for long-term health and vitality, these power-packed snacks will leave you feeling full, satisfied, and, above all, well nourished.

ON THE GO

Want to have a few snacks on you when you're out and about? This chapter includes an array of delicious and easily portable snacks for eating on the go.

GRAPE & LYCHEE REVIVER JUICE

The combination of fragrant lychees and creamy avocado in this juice make it the perfect pick-me-up to rehydrate and fight fatigue.

SERVES: 1   PREP: 10–15 MINS   CHILL: NO CHILLING

2 cups green grapes

2 cups baby spinach

½ ripe avocado, pitted and flesh scooped from the skin, plus a slice to serve (optional)

5 lychees, peeled and pitted

small handful of crushed ice

½ cup chilled water

1. Feed the grapes and spinach through a juicer.

2. Pour the juice into a blender, add the avocado, lychees, and crushed ice, and process until smooth.

3. Add the water and process again.

4. Pour into a glass, add the avocado slice (if using), and serve immediately.

10

per serving: 413 cal / 15.6g fat
2.1g sat fat / 72.8g carbs / 54.6g sugars
0.1g salt / 11.2g fiber / 6.3g protein

SPICE-ROASTED EDAMAME & CRANBERRIES

Frozen edamame, or young soybeans, make a healthy, protein-packed snack, and their high levels of fiber keep you feeling fuller, longer.

SERVES: 4　　　PREP: 15 MINS, PLUS COOLING　　　COOK: 15 MINS

2 cups frozen edamame (soybeans)

2-inch piece fresh ginger, peeled and finely grated

1 teaspoon Sichuan peppercorns, coarsely crushed

1 tablespoon soy sauce

1 tablespoon olive oil

3 small star anise

⅓ cup dried cranberries

per serving: 179 cal / 9.1g fat
1g sat fat / 12.2g carbs / 7.3g sugars
0.5g salt / 4.3g fiber / 11.1g protein

1. Preheat the oven to 350°F. Put the edamame into a roasting pan, then sprinkle with the ginger and peppercorns, drizzle with soy sauce and oil, and mix together.

2. Tuck the star anise in among the edamame, then roast, uncovered, in the preheated oven for 15 minutes.

3. Stir in the cranberries and let cool. Spoon into a small container and eat within 12 hours.

12

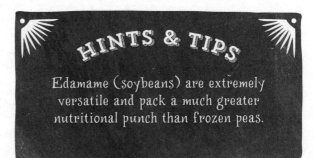

HINTS & TIPS

Edamame (soybeans) are extremely versatile and pack a much greater nutritional punch than frozen peas.

SQUASH & PUMPKIN SEED MUFFINS

With just a hint of sweetness, these gingery muffins taste delicious
still warm from the oven with a generous spreading of butter.

MAKES: 12   PREP: 25–30 MINS, PLUS COOLING   COOK: 30 MINS

light olive oil, for oiling
2 cups peeled and seeded
½-inch butternut squash dice
1½-inch piece fresh ginger,
scrubbed and coarsely grated
3 eggs
¼ cup maple syrup
1 cup low-fat plain yogurt
1¼ cups whole-wheat flour
¾ cup fine cornmeal
1 tablespoon baking powder
1 teaspoon ground pumpkin
pie spice
3 tablespoons pumpkin seeds
(pepita)

per muffin: 144 cal / 3.7g fat
1g sat fat / 23.3g carbs / 5.8g sugars
0.9g salt / 1.6g fiber / 5.7g protein

14

1. Preheat the oven to 375°F. Lightly brush a 12-cup muffin pan with oil.

2. Put the diced squash into the top of a steamer set over a saucepan of gently simmering water, cover, and cook for 15 minutes, until just soft. Mash and mix with the grated ginger.

3. Put the eggs, maple syrup, and yogurt into a medium bowl and whisk together.

4. Put the flour, cornmeal, baking powder, and pumpkin pie spice into a larger bowl and stir together, then add the mashed squash and egg mix, and briefly whisk together until just combined.

5. Spoon the batter into the prepared pan, sprinkle the tops with the seeds, then bake in the preheated oven for 15 minutes, until well risen and golden brown. Let cool in the pan for 5 minutes, then loosen the edges with a knife, turn out onto a wire rack, and let cool completely. These are best eaten within two days of making.

MIXED QUINOA BALLS

One recipe, three flavors—these super-power balls are a great get-ahead snack. Cook up a big batch to carry on the go.

MAKES: 24   PREP: 35 MINS, PLUS CHILLING   COOK: 35 MINS

⅔ cup quinoa
1½ cups boiling water
3 tomatoes, halved
2 garlic cloves, finely chopped
2 teaspoons torn fresh thyme
2 tablespoons virgin olive oil
4 cups baby spinach, rinsed and drained
1 cup drained and finely crumbled feta cheese
pinch of grated nutmeg
¼ cup pitted ripe black olives, finely chopped
1 tablespoon chopped fresh basil
sea salt and pepper, to taste
sweet chili relish, to serve (optional)

per ball: 52 cal / 3.1g fat
1.3g sat fat / 4.3g carbs / 0.8g sugars
0.3g salt / 1.9g fiber / 2g protein

1. Add the quinoa and water to a medium saucepan, cover, and cook over medium heat for about 20 minutes, stirring occasionally, until the quinoa is soft and has absorbed all the water.

2. Meanwhile, preheat the broiler. Arrange the tomatoes, cut-side up, on the bottom of an aluminum foil-lined broiler rack. Sprinkle with the garlic, thyme, and a little salt and pepper, then drizzle with 1 tablespoon of the oil and broil for 10 minutes.

3. Add the spinach to a dry, nonstick skillet and cook for 2–3 minutes, until just wilted. Scoop out of the pan and finely chop, then mix with one-third of the quinoa, one-third of the cheese, a little nutmeg, and salt and pepper.

4. Peel the tomatoes, chop, and add with any pan juices to the empty spinach pan. Stir in half the remaining quinoa and cook for 2–3 minutes, until the mixture is dry enough to shape into a ball. Remove from the heat and stir in half the remaining cheese.

5. Mix the remaining quinoa and cheese with the olives, basil, and a little salt and pepper. Shape each of the flavored quinoa mixtures into eight small balls. Chill until ready to serve.

6. Preheat the oven to 350°F. Brush a roasting pan with the remaining oil, add the quinoa balls, and bake for 10 minutes, turning once, until the edges are golden brown and the cheese has melted. Serve hot or cold with sweet chili relish, if using, for dipping. Transfer the cooled quinoa balls to an airtight plastic container, refrigerate, and eat within three days.

MIXED NUTS IN HERBED SALT

Simple to make and wonderfully tasty, these addictive pan-roasted nuts are bursting with protein, healthy fats, and loads of flavor.

SERVES: 4   PREP: 10 MINS, PLUS COOLING   COOK: 5 MINS

1 tablespoon olive oil

2 fresh rosemary sprigs, leaves torn from the stems

½ cup cashew nuts

½ cup pecans

½ cup unblanched almonds

½ cup unblanched hazelnuts

½ teaspoon sea salt

per serving: 366 cal / 34.4g fat
3.5g sat fat / 11.3g carbs / 2.5g sugars
0.7g salt / 4.8g fiber / 8.7g protein

1. Heat the oil and rosemary in a medium skillet, then swirl the oil around the pan to flavor it with the rosemary. Add the nuts and cook over medium heat for 2–3 minutes, until lightly toasted.

2. Stir in the salt, then spoon the nuts into a bowl and let cool before eating. Any leftover nuts can be stored in a sealed plastic container or jar in the refrigerator for up the three days.

SPICE IT UP

Instead of rosemary, try a little curry powder or a blend of ground turmeric, garam masala, smoked paprika, and a pinch of chili powder.

On the go

EDAMAME

A common ingredient in Japanese cuisine, edamame are the immature, green soybeans still in the pod. Typically, the beans are boiled and served with salt.

LYCHEES

Lychees are a subtropical fruit native to China. They feature significantly in traditional Chinese medicine, because all parts of the fruit, including its flesh, seeds, bark, root, and flowers, have health benefits.

BEETS

The earthy sweetness of beets and their impressive nutrients are beginning to make them a more popular choice. Don't overlook the beet greens—they can be cooked in the same way as you would cook spinach.

PUMPKIN SEEDS

Containing high amounts of zinc and magnesium, pumpkin seeds, or pepita, are one of the most versatile superfoods you can incorporate into your diet.

APRICOTS

Like peaches and plums, apricots are members of the rose family. They are rich in vitamin A and a good source of vitamin C, potassium, and dietary fiber.

ALMONDS

Bursting with healthy fats and protein, almonds are among the most valuable superfoods. Choose almonds with the skins on (instead of blanched), because these contain the highest concentration of nutrients.

ROOT VEGETABLE CHIPS WITH HERB YOGURT DIP

Making your own chips is surprisingly easy, and you can be certain there are no added artificial flavorings or preservatives.

SERVES: 4   PREP: 30–35 MINS, PLUS COOLING   COOK: 12–16 MINS

2¼ pounds mixed root vegetables, such as carrots, parsnips, sweet potatoes, or beets, thinly sliced
¼ cup virgin olive oil
sea salt and pepper, to taste

HERB YOGURT DIP
1 cup Greek-style plain yogurt
2 garlic cloves, finely chopped
¼ cup finely chopped fresh herbs, such as flat-leaf parsley, chives, basil, or oregano

per serving: 320 cal / 9.6g fat
1.1g sat fat / 37.7g carbs / 14.7g sugars
1.8g salt / 8.4g fiber / 7.8g protein

22

1. Preheat the oven to 400°F. To make the herb yogurt dip, spoon the yogurt into a small bowl, then stir in the garlic and herbs, and season with salt and pepper. Cover and chill in the refrigerator until ready to serve.

2. Put the vegetables into a large bowl. Slowly drizzle with the oil, gently turning the vegetables as you go, until they are thoroughly coated.

3. Arrange the vegetables over three baking sheets in a single layer, then season with salt and pepper. Bake for 8–10 minutes, then check—the slices in the corners of the sheets will cook more quickly, so transfer any that are crisp and golden to a wire rack. Cook the rest for an additional 2–3 minutes, then transfer any more cooked chips to the wire rack. Cook the remaining slices for an additional 2–3 minutes, if needed, then transfer any remaining chips to the wire rack and let cool.

4. Arrange the chips in a bowl and spoon the dip into a smaller bowl to serve. Any leftover chips can be stored in an airtight container for up to two days.

SMOKY PAPRIKA ROASTED CHICKPEAS

Chickpeas are made up of complex carbohydrates, which take longer for the body to digest and so provide a slower release of energy.

SERVES: 4   PREP: 15 MINS, PLUS COOLING   COOK: 18–24 MINS

2 tablespoons olive oil

1 teaspoon cumin seeds, coarsely crushed

1 teaspoon smoked mild paprika

¼ teaspoon ground allspice

¼ teaspoon ground cinnamon

½ teaspoon sea salt

2 (15-ounce) cans chickpeas in water, drained

2 tablespoons date syrup

per serving: 235 cal / 8.3g fat
1g sat fat / 36g carbs / 6.5g sugars
0.8g salt / 5.7g fiber / 7.2g protein

1. Preheat the oven to 400°F. Add the oil to a roasting pan and place in the oven to heat for 3–4 minutes.

2. Add the cumin seeds, paprika, allspice, cinnamon, and salt to a small bowl, and mix together well.

3. Add the chickpeas to the roasting pan, drizzle with the date syrup, sprinkle with the spice mix, and stir together. Roast in the preheated oven for 15–20 minutes, stirring once, until brown and crusty.

4. Spoon into a bowl and let cool before eating. Store any leftovers in a tightly sealed plastic container or jar in the refrigerator for up to three days.

24

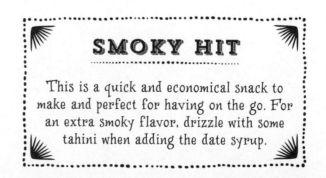

SMOKY HIT

This is a quick and economical snack to make and perfect for having on the go. For an extra smoky flavor, drizzle with some tahini when adding the date syrup.

FRUIT & NUT TRAIL MIX

Trail mix must be an all-time favorite snack, and this recipe is filled with energy-boosting, fiber-rich fruit, nuts, and seeds.

SERVES: 12   **PREP: 10 MINS**   **COOK: NO COOKING**

⅔ cup chopped dried apricots
⅔ cup dried cranberries
¾ cup roasted cashew nuts
¾ cup shelled hazelnuts
⅔ cup shelled and halved Brazil nuts
¾ cup slivered almonds
¼ cup toasted pumpkin seeds (pepita)
¼ cup sunflower seeds
¼ cup toasted pine nuts

per serving: 261 cal / 20.6g fat
2.7g sat fat / 17g carbs / 9.8g sugars
trace salt / 3.6g fiber / 6.9g protein

1. Put all the ingredients into an airtight container, close the lid, and shake several times. Shake the container before each opening, then reseal. This mix will stay fresh for up to two weeks if tightly sealed.

CHEWY APRICOT & ALMOND ENERGY BARS

These oat-filled, dairy-free energy bars are great for carrying with you for a healthy midmorning snack.

MAKES: 15 **PREP: 25 MINS, PLUS COOLING** **COOK: 30 MINS**

½ cup coconut oil

⅓ cup firmly packed light brown sugar

¼ cup almond butter, or other nut butter

1 crisp, sweet apple, cored and coarsely grated

1⅔ cups rolled oats

⅓ cup brown rice flour

½ cup unblanched almonds, coarsely chopped

⅓ cup sunflower seeds

1½ cups dried apricots, diced

per bar: 235 cal / 14g fat
7.2g sat fat / 26.6g carbs / 14.6g sugars
trace salt / 3.5g fiber / 4.2g protein

1. Preheat the oven to 350°F. Line an 8-inch square shallow cake pan with nonstick parchment paper.

2. Heat the oil and sugar in a medium saucepan over low heat until the oil has melted and the sugar has dissolved. Remove from the heat and stir in the almond butter until melted.

3. Add the apple, oats, flour, almonds, and sunflower seeds, and mix together well.

4. Spoon two-thirds of the mixture into the prepared pan and press down firmly. Sprinkle with the apricots and press firmly into the bottom layer, then dot the remaining oat mixture over the top in a thin layer so that some of the apricots are still visible.

5. Bake in the preheated oven for about 25 minutes, until the top is golden brown. Remove from the oven and let cool in the pan until almost cold, then cut into 15 small rectangles. Let cool completely, then lift the bars out of the pan, using the paper. Separate the bars and pack into a plastic container. Store in the refrigerator for up to three days.

29

NO WHEAT

These tasty bars are wheat-free, but do check the oats carefully. Some brands may be contaminated with other wheat or gluten cereals during harvesting and milling.

SUPERSEEDY GRANOLA

Traditionally thought of as a breakfast cereal with milk, granola also makes a crunchy, sweet-tasting snack served on its own.

SERVES: 6   PREP: 20 MINS, PLUS COOLING   COOK: 30–35 MINS

1⅔ cups rolled oats
¼ cup pumpkin seeds (pepita)
¼ cup sunflower seeds
¼ cup sesame seeds
1 teaspoon ground cinnamon
2 tablespoons packed light brown sugar
2 tablespoons olive oil
2 tablespoons honey
juice of 1 small orange
½ cup diced dried apple slices
⅓ cup dried blueberries
¼ cup dried cranberries

per serving: 358 cal / 16.3g fat
2.2g sat fat / 48g carbs / 23.5g sugars
trace salt / 6.2g fiber / 12.3g protein

1. Preheat the oven to 325°F. Add the rolled oats, pumpkin seeds, sunflower seeds, and sesame seeds to a 7 x 11-inch roasting pan. Sprinkle with the cinnamon and sugar, and stir together.

2. Drizzle the oil, honey, and orange juice over the top and mix together. Bake in the preheated oven for 30–35 minutes, stirring after 15 minutes, moving the mix in the corners to the center because the edges will brown more quickly. Try to keep the granola in clumps. Return to the oven and stir every 5–10 minutes, until the granola is an even, golden brown.

3. Sprinkle the dried apple, blueberries, and cranberries over the top and let the granola cool and harden. Spoon into a tightly sealed plastic container or jar and store in the refrigerator for up to four days.

MIX & MATCH

Vary the types of seeds or omit them and replace with your favorite nuts—unblanched, coarsely chopped almonds or whole hazelnuts work well.

TAKE TO WORK

This chapter contains nutritious and filling
snacks that are ideal for taking to work—
and they'll keep you away from the
vending machine, too.

ROASTED KALE CHIPS

Kale's flavor becomes wonderfully intense when the leaves are roasted. These chips are perfect on their own or sprinkled over soup.

SERVES: 4   PREP: 20 MINS   COOK: 10–12 MINS

8 ounces kale
2 tablespoons olive oil
2 pinches of sugar
2 pinches of sea salt
2 tablespoons toasted slivered almonds, to garnish

per serving: 122 cal / 9.6g fat
1.1g sat fat / 8.1g carbs / 1.2g sugars
0.4g salt / 1.7g fiber / 3g protein

1. Preheat the oven to 300°F. Remove the thick stems and the central ribs from the kale leaves. Rinse and dry thoroughly with paper towels. Tear into bite-size pieces and put into a bowl with the oil and sugar, then toss well.

2. Spread about half the leaves in a single layer in a large roasting pan, spaced well apart. Sprinkle with a pinch of salt and roast on the bottom rack of the preheated oven for 4 minutes.

3. Stir the leaves, then turn the pan so the back is at the front. Roast for an additional 1–2 minutes, until the leaves are crisp and slightly browned at the edges. Repeat with the remaining leaves and salt. Sprinkle the kale chips with the slivered almonds to serve.

TOP TIP

It's important to put the roasting pan on the bottom rack of the oven, where the heat is gentler. The leaves can easily burn, so check them often.

RAINBOW NORI ROLLS

Full of protective antioxidants and vitamins, these colorful snacks can be filled with any combination of vegetables you prefer.

SERVES: 4   PREP: 30–35 MINS, PLUS COOLING   COOK: 27–30 MINS

1 cup glutinous or risotto rice

3 cups cold water

2 tablespoons mirin (Japanese rice wine) or sherry

1 tablespoon light olive oil

24 asparagus tips

4 sheets nori

1 cup drained, sliced sushi ginger

⅓ cup thin kale strips

1 small red bell pepper, halved, seeded, and cut into thin strips

1 small yellow bell pepper, halved, seeded, and cut into thin strips

2 carrots, cut into matchstick strips

2 cooked beets in natural juices, drained and cut into matchstick strips

2 tablespoons tamari

2 tablespoons Chinese rice wine

sea salt

per serving: 235 cal / 4.1g fat
0.5g sat fat / 41.6g carbs / 9g sugars
4.3g salt / 4.9g fiber / 6.2g protein

1. Put the rice and water into a saucepan with a little salt and bring to a boil, stirring occasionally. Reduce the heat and gently simmer for 18–20 minutes, or according to the package directions, until the rice is soft and has absorbed all the water. Stir occasionally toward the end of cooking so the rice doesn't stick to the bottom of the pan. Remove from the heat and stir in the mirin or sherry. Let cool for 10 minutes.

2. Heat the oil in a skillet, add the asparagus, and sauté over medium heat for 3–4 minutes, until just soft, then set aside.

3. Separate the nori sheets and place one on a piece of plastic wrap set on top of a bamboo sushi mat. Thinly spread one-quarter of the warm rice over the top to cover the nori sheet completely.

4. Arrange one-quarter of the ginger in an overlapping line a little up from one edge of the nori. Arrange one-quarter of the asparagus and kale next to it, then one-quarter of the red and yellow bell peppers, followed by one-quarter of the carrot and beets, leaving a border of rice about ¾ inch wide.

5. Using the plastic wrap and sushi mat, tightly roll the nori around the vegetables. Remove the bamboo mat, then twist the ends of the plastic and place the roll on a tray. Repeat to make three more nori rolls, then chill for 1 hour, or longer if preferred.

6. To serve, mix the tamari and rice wine together, then spoon into four small dipping bowls and set the bowls on serving plates. Unwrap each nori roll and cut into five thick slices. These are best eaten on the day they are made.

37

CHEESY FLAXSEED & QUINOA CRACKERS WITH TOMATO SALSA

These crackers are made with gluten-free quinoa flour and flaxseed, so they're ideal for those on a wheat- or gluten-free diet.

SERVES: 4   PREP: 35 MINS, PLUS COOLING   COOK: 12–15 MINS

¼ cup flaxseed, plus
1 tablespoon for sprinkling
1 cup quinoa flour
½ teaspoon dry mustard
¼ teaspoon sea salt
pinch of cayenne pepper
4 tablespoons butter, diced
½ cup shredded sharp
cheddar cheese
2 eggs, 1 beaten, 1 separated
1 tablespoon sesame seeds

SALSA
2 tomatoes, cut into wedges
1 scallion, sliced
2-3 fresh cilantro sprigs
sea salt and cayenne pepper,
to taste

per serving: 378 cal / 25.5g fat
11.5g sat fat / 24.3g carbs / 1.9g sugars
1.7g salt / 5.9g fiber / 13.7g protein

1. Preheat the oven to 375°F. Grind the ¼ cup of flaxseed in a spice mill to a coarse flour, then transfer to a bowl and stir in the quinoa flour, dry mustard, salt, and cayenne pepper.

2. Add the butter and rub in with your fingertips until the mixture resembles fine crumbs. Stir in the cheese, then mix in the egg and egg yolk, and press together with your hands to make a coarse dough.

3. Gently knead the dough, then place between two sheets of nonstick parchment paper, roll out to a rectangle, and trim to 10 x 8 inches. Cut into 1 x 4-inch crackers. Leaving the crackers on the paper, separate them slightly, then slide a baking sheet under the paper.

4. Lightly beat the egg white, then brush it over the crackers and sprinkle with the remaining tablespoon of flaxseed and the sesame seeds. Bake in the preheated oven for 12–15 minutes, until golden, then let cool on the paper.

5. Meanwhile, make the salsa by finely chopping the tomatoes, scallion, and cilantro. Season with salt and cayenne pepper, and spoon into a small bowl. Set out with the crackers to serve. These are best eaten on the day they are made.

39

SUPERSEEDS

Flaxseed, sometimes called linseed, contain more minerals than any other seeds. Grinding or crushing them means the body is better able to absorb their nutrients.

ZUCCHINI & WALNUT ROLLS

It will be hard to resist the wonderful smell of these little rolls. Serve warm just as they are, with a little butter or soft goat cheese.

MAKES: 8   **PREP: 25 MINS, PLUS RISING**   **COOK: 10–12 MINS**

olive oil, for oiling

3½ cups multigrain or whole-wheat flour, plus extra for dusting

1 teaspoon caraway seeds

1 teaspoon sea salt

2 tablespoons packed brown sugar

2 tablespoons butter

2 teaspoons active dry yeast

2 cups shredded zucchini

⅔ cup lukewarm water

½ cup coarsely chopped walnut pieces

per roll: 297 cal / 9.9g fat
2.5g sat fat / 47.4g carbs / 4.2g sugars
trace salt / 7.1g fiber / 9.3g protein

1. Line two baking sheets with parchment paper.

2. Put the flour, caraway seeds, salt, sugar, and butter into a mixing bowl and rub in the butter until the mixture resembles fine crumbs. Stir in the yeast.

3. Mix in the zucchini, then add the warm water and mix to a soft dough. Turn out onto a lightly floured surface, add the walnuts, and knead for about 5 minutes, until the dough is smooth and elastic.

4. Cut the dough into eight pieces, then place on the prepared baking sheets. Loosely cover the tops with a piece of oiled plastic wrap and let rest in a warm place for 45 minutes–1 hour, or until the dough has risen.

5. Meanwhile, preheat the oven to 425°F. Remove the plastic wrap, dust the tops of the rolls with a little flour, and bake in the preheated oven for 10–12 minutes, until golden brown and the bread sounds hollow when tapped on the bottom. Turn out onto a wire rack to cool before serving. Once cooled, store leftover rolls in an airtight container for up to two days.

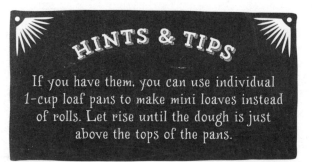

HINTS & TIPS

If you have them, you can use individual 1-cup loaf pans to make mini loaves instead of rolls. Let rise until the dough is just above the tops of the pans.

GOAT CHEESE TRUFFLES WITH HONEY & PISTACHIO CRUMB

Made in practically no time, these tasty, high-protein truffles are delicious served straight from the refrigerator.

MAKES: 12   PREP: 15 MINS, PLUS CHILLING   COOK: NO COOKING

5½ ounces French rindless soft goat cheese

1 teaspoon honey

⅓ cup pistachio nuts, finely chopped

sea salt and pepper, to taste

per truffle: 54 cal / 4.1g fat
2g sat fat / 1.5g carbs / 0.8g sugars
0.4g salt / 0.3g fiber / 3g protein

1. Mix the cheese and honey with a little salt and pepper in a bowl.

2. Scoop heaping teaspoons of the mixture onto a plate to make about 12 mounds.

3. Sprinkle the nuts over a separate, smaller plate, then roll one mound of cheese at a time in the nuts until evenly coated and shaped like a ball. Place on a plate and chill in the refrigerator for 1 hour before serving. Pack any leftover truffles into a small plastic container and store in the refrigerator for up to three days.

Take to work

PISTACHIOS

Pistachios are in fact seeds, not nuts, and come from a tree in the cashew family. Like most seeds, pistachios have an impressive fat profile, so watch your portion size to avoid a skyrocketing calorie count.

HONEY

Honey and, in particular New Zealand Manuka honey, has been shown to have potent antibacterial properties as well as an anti-inflammatory action that can quickly reduce pain once applied.

MEDJOOL DATES

Dates are a natural source of sweetness and make a great replacement for sugar. They also pack a nutritional punch, containing plenty of fiber, potassium, manganese, and vitamins A, B_6, and K.

TOMATOES

Tomatoes get their red color from lycopene, a carotenoid pigment which, along with other antioxidants, may help protect against free-radical damage and prevent blood clots.

QUINOA

Native to Peru and Bolivia, this "supergrain" is said to be the only plant food that contains all essential amino acids, putting it on a par with animal protein.

KALE

When in doubt, go for green. As well as containing high levels of vitamin C, folic acid, and iron, the deep green pigment chlorophyll in green vegetables assists with the oxygenation and health of blood cells.

ROSEMARY, SEA SALT & SESAME POPCORN

Forget about fat- and additive-laden potato chips; popcorn can be cooked in a fraction of the oil for a healthier alternative.

SERVES: 4   PREP: 10–15 MINS   COOK: 6–8 MINS

⅓ cup sesame seeds
2 tablespoons olive oil
2 rosemary stems, torn into large pieces
1 cup popping corn
1 teaspoon sea salt
2 tablespoons balsamic vinegar, or to taste

per serving: 79 cal / 25.2g fat
3.2g sat fat / 30g carbs / 1.6g sugars
1.5g salt / 6.6g fiber / 6.4g protein

46

1. Add the sesame seeds to a large skillet with 1 teaspoon of the oil, cover, and cook over medium heat for 2–3 minutes, shaking the pan from time to time, until the seeds are toasted golden brown and beginning to pop. Scoop out of the pan into a bowl and wipe out the pan with a piece of paper towel.

2. Add the remaining oil and the rosemary to the pan and heat gently, shaking the pan to release the rosemary's oil. Add the corn, cover with the lid, and cook over medium heat for 3–4 minutes, shaking the pan, until all the popcorn has popped.

3. Remove from the heat, sprinkle with the toasted sesame seeds and season with the salt and vinegar, then transfer to a serving bowl, discarding the rosemary just before eating.

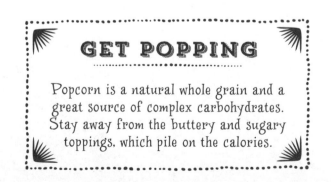

GET POPPING

Popcorn is a natural whole grain and a great source of complex carbohydrates. Stay away from the buttery and sugary toppings, which pile on the calories.

COCONUT, CACAO & HAZELNUT TRUFFLES

These little power-packed balls are just bursting with a nutritious mix of vital minerals, vitamins, protein, and raw ingredients.

MAKES: 20   **PREP: 25 MINS**   **COOK: NO COOKING**

¾ cup unblanched hazelnuts

⅓ cup cacao nibs, plus 1 tablespoon for coating

6 dried figs, coarsely chopped

⅓ cup dried coconut flakes, plus 2 tablespoons for coating

1 tablespoon maple syrup

finely grated zest and juice of ½ small orange

per truffle: 46 cal / 3.5g fat
1g sat fat / 3.2g carbs / 2.1g sugars
trace salt / 0.9g fiber / 1.3g protein

1. Add the hazelnuts and the ⅓ cup of cacao nibs to a food processor and process until finely chopped.

2. Add the figs, the ⅓ cup of coconut, maple syrup, and orange zest and juice to the processor, and process until finely chopped and the mixture has come together in a ball.

3. Scoop the mixture out of the food processor, then cut into 20 even pieces. Roll into small balls between the palms of your hands.

4. Finely chop the extra cacao nibs, then mix with the extra coconut on a sheet of parchment paper or a plate. Roll the truffles, one at a time, in the cacao and coconut mixture, then arrange in a small plastic container. Store in the refrigerator for up to three days.

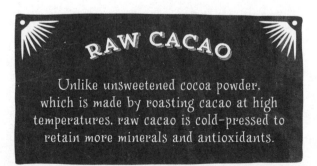

RAW CACAO

Unlike unsweetened cocoa powder, which is made by roasting cacao at high temperatures, raw cacao is cold-pressed to retain more minerals and antioxidants.

WHOLE-WHEAT MUFFINS

These muffins are made with whole-wheat flour and packed with fiber-rich fruit and oats—perfect for a treat.

MAKES: 10   PREP: 20–25 MINS, PLUS COOLING   COOK: 25–30 MINS

2 cups whole-wheat flour
2 teaspoons baking powder
2 tablespoons packed light brown sugar
¾ cup finely chopped dried apricots
1 banana, mashed with 1 tablespoon orange juice
1 teaspoon finely grated orange zest
1¼ cups skim milk
1 egg, beaten
3 tablespoons canola or sunflower oil
2 tablespoons rolled oats
honey or maple syrup, to serve (optional)

1. Preheat the oven to 400°F. Put ten muffin cups into a muffin pan. Sift the flour and baking powder into a mixing bowl, adding any husks that remain in the sifter. Stir in the sugar and chopped apricots.

2. Make a well in the center of the dry ingredients and add the banana, orange zest, milk, beaten egg, and oil. Mix together well to form a thick batter. Divide the batter evenly among the ten muffin cups.

3. Sprinkle each muffin with a few rolled oats and bake in the preheated oven for 25–30 minutes, or until well risen and firm to the touch. Transfer the muffins to a wire rack to cool slightly. Serve the muffins warm with a little honey or maple syrup, if using. Store the cooled muffins in an airtight plastic container for 2–3 days.

51

per muffin: 185 cal / 5.5g fat
0.6g sat fat / 30.8g carbs / 11.1g sugars
0.7g salt / 3.7g fiber / 5.4g protein

CHOCOLATE BROWNIE QUINOA COOKIES

Quinoa flour is made by grinding quinoa seeds and is a great grain- and gluten-free alternative to wheat flours.

MAKES: 26   **PREP: 30 MINS, PLUS CHILLING**   **COOK: 12–14 MINS**

¼ cup coconut oil

4 ounces bittersweet chocolate, chopped

½ cup quinoa flour

1 tablespoon unsweetened cocoa powder

1 teaspoon baking soda

½ teaspoon ground cinnamon

2 eggs

⅔ cup firmly packed light brown sugar

1 teaspoon natural vanilla extract

per cookie: 78 cal / 4.3g fat
3g sat fat / 9.1g carbs / 7.1g sugars
trace salt / 0.7g fiber / 1.2g protein

1. Preheat the oven to 375°F. Line three baking sheets with nonstick parchment paper.

2. Put the oil and chocolate into a heatproof bowl and set over a saucepan of gently simmering water, making sure that the bowl is not touching the water. Heat for 5 minutes, or until the chocolate has melted, then stir to mix.

3. Add the quinoa flour, cocoa powder, baking soda, and cinnamon to a separate bowl and stir together.

4. Add the eggs, sugar, and vanilla extract to a large mixing bowl and whisk together until thick and frothy. Gently fold in the oil-and-chocolate mixture, then add the flour mixture and stir until smooth.

5. Drop tablespoons of the brownie mixture onto the prepared sheets, spaced well apart, then bake in the preheated oven for 7–9 minutes, until crusty and cracked, and still slightly soft to the touch. Let cool and harden slightly on the sheets, then lift off the paper and pack into an airtight container. Eat within three days.

53

RAW DATE & COCONUT BARS

These chunky, nutty bars get the most out of power-packed raw ingredients. Perfect to keep you energized at work all afternoon long.

MAKES: 12   PREP: 30 MINS, PLUS CHILLING   COOK: NO COOKING

3 cups halved and pitted medjool dates

⅔ cup unblanched almonds

⅔ cup cashew nuts

2 tablespoons chia seeds

2 tablespoons maca powder

2 teaspoons natural vanilla extract

¼ cup dried coconut flakes

½ cup coarsely chopped unblanched hazelnuts

¼ cup pecan halves

per bar: 225 cal / 11g fat
2g sat fat / 31.7g carbs / 23.5g sugars
trace salt / 5.4g fiber / 4.2g protein

1. Add the dates, almonds, and cashew nuts to a food processor and process until finely chopped.

2. Add the chia seeds, maca powder, and vanilla extract, and process until the mixture binds together to form a coarse ball.

3. Tear off two sheets of nonstick parchment paper, put one on the work surface, and sprinkle with half the coconut flakes. Put the date ball on top, then press into a rectangle with your fingertips. Cover with the second sheet of paper and roll out to a 12 x 8-inch rectangle. Lift off the top piece of paper, sprinkle with the remaining coconut, the hazelnuts, and pecans, then replace the paper and briefly roll with a rolling pin to press the nuts into the date mixture.

4. Loosen the top paper, then transfer the date mixture, still on the bottom paper, to a tray and chill for 3 hours or overnight, until firm.

5. Remove the top paper, cut the date mixture into 12 pieces, peel off the bottom paper, then pack into a plastic container, layering with pieces of parchment paper to keep them separate. Store in the refrigerator for up to three days.

54

HIGH ENERGY

Part of leading a healthy, sustainable lifestyle
is regular exercise, and these superhealthy
snacks are high in protein and healthy fats
to give you optimum amounts of energy.

APPLE & PEANUT BUTTER SANDWICHES

These fruity "sandwiches" are the perfect pre-workout snack for loads of energy, minus the processed, wheat- and gluten-heavy bread.

SERVES: 4 **PREP: 20 MINS** **COOK: NO COOKING**

2 green crisp, sweet apples
2 red crisp, sweet apples
juice of 2 lemons
½ cup chunky peanut butter
¼ cup dried cranberries, coarsely chopped
2 tablespoons sunflower seeds
2 tablespoons rolled oats
½ cup diced dried apricots
⅓ cup coarsely chopped unblanched hazelnuts

per serving: 468 cal / 23.4g fat
3g sat fat / 63.5g carbs / 43.1g sugars
trace salt / 10.7g fiber / 11g protein

1. Cut each apple into six slices, then remove any seeds (there is no need to core them). Put the apple pieces into a bowl, add the lemon juice, and turn to coat evenly to prevent discoloration.

2. Drain the apples, place on a tray or cutting board, and spread each slice with peanut butter. Sprinkle half the slices with the cranberries, sunflower seeds, oats, apricots, and hazelnuts.

3. Cover with the remaining apple slices, peanut butter-side downward, and press together to make fruity sandwiches. Serve immediately.

58

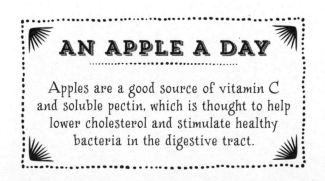

AN APPLE A DAY

Apples are a good source of vitamin C and soluble pectin, which is thought to help lower cholesterol and stimulate healthy bacteria in the digestive tract.

PROTEIN BERRY WHIP

Frozen berries are a healthy and handy pantry staple. Process with protein-boosting cashew and Brazil nuts for a delicious shake.

SERVES: 4   PREP: 10–15 MINS   COOK: NO COOKING

2 cups frozen mixed sliced strawberries and blueberries
4 Brazil nuts
⅓ cup cashew nuts
¼ cup rolled oats
2 cups almond milk
2 tablespoons maple syrup

per serving: 213 cal / 12.8g fat
2.4g sat fat / 23.2g carbs / 11.6g sugars
0.2g salt / 3.5g fiber / 4.7g protein

1. Put the frozen berries, Brazil nuts, and cashew nuts into a blender or food processor. Sprinkle with the oats, then pour in half the almond milk. Process until smooth.

2. Add the remaining milk and maple syrup, and process again until smooth. Pour into four glasses and serve immediately with spoons. As the drink stands, the blueberries will almost set the liquid, but as soon as you stir it, it will turn to liquid again.

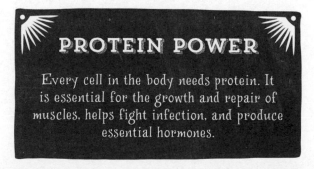

PROTEIN POWER

Every cell in the body needs protein. It is essential for the growth and repair of muscles, helps fight infection, and produce essential hormones.

TURKEY & RAINBOW CHARD ROLL-UPS

Rainbow chard has the most beautiful pink, red, yellow, or white stems and makes a nutritious alternative to kale.

MAKES: 8	PREP: 30 MINS	COOK: NO COOKING

8 rainbow chard leaves and stems (choose leaves that are about the same size as the slices of turkey)

1 avocado, halved and pitted

juice of 1 lemon

8 thin slices cooked turkey

⅔ cup hummus

2 scallions, trimmed and cut into fine strips

1 carrot, cut into matchstick strips

1 small zucchini, cut into matchstick strips

per roll-up: 104 cal / 6.1g fat
1g sat fat / 7.5g carbs / 1.6g sugars
0.5g salt / 3.6g fiber / 6.5g protein

1. Cut the stems from the chard leaves, then cut the stems into thin matchstick strips and set aside. Peel the avocado and cut into long, thin slices, then toss in the lemon juice and set aside.

2. Separate the chard leaves and arrange, shiny-side down, on a large cutting board. Cover each one with a slice of turkey, then spread the turkey with a little hummus.

3. Divide the chard stems, scallions, carrot, and zucchini among the chard leaves, making a little pile on each leaf that runs in the center of the leaf from long edge to long edge.

4. Top the little mounds with the avocado slices, then roll up from the bottom of the leaf to the tip and put on a plate, seam downward. Continue until all the leaves have been rolled.

5. Cut each roll into thick slices and transfer to individual plates, or wrap each roll in plastic wrap and chill for up to 1 hour. Don't keep them for longer, because the avocado will begin to discolor.

EAT MORE VEG

Sneaking raw vegetables into energy-boosting snacks like this is the easiest way to increase your vitamin intake. Any combination of vegetables will do.

LOADED SWEET POTATOES

This veggy version of a baked potato is topped with Middle-Eastern spiced chickpeas and tomatoes for a light but mighty refueling snack.

SERVES: 4　　　PREP: 20–25 MINS　　　COOK: 50–55 MINS

4 small sweet potatoes, scrubbed
1 tablespoon olive oil
1 small onion, chopped
1 garlic clove, finely chopped
1 teaspoon ground coriander
½ teaspoon ground cumin
2 tomatoes, peeled and diced
2 teaspoons tomato paste
1¼ cups drained, canned chickpeas
¼ cup chopped fresh cilantro
½ cup fat-free Greek-style yogurt
sea salt and pepper, to taste

per serving: 257 cal / 4.2g fat
0.5g sat fat / 47.8g carbs / 9.8g sugars
0.9g salt / 8.1g fiber / 8.4g protein

64

1. Preheat the oven to 375°F. Prick the sweet potatoes with a fork, put them on a baking sheet, and bake in the preheated oven for 45–50 minutes, or until they feel soft when squeezed.

2. Meanwhile, heat the oil in a small skillet, add the onion, and sauté over medium heat for 4–5 minutes, until soft. Stir in the garlic, ground coriander, and cumin, and cook for an additional minute.

3. Mix in the tomatoes, tomato paste, and chickpeas, then season with a little salt and pepper. Cover and cook for 10 minutes, then remove from the heat and set aside.

4. Transfer the potatoes to a serving plate, cut each along its length and open out slightly. Reheat the chickpeas and spoon them over the potatoes. Mix half the fresh cilantro into the yogurt and spoon it over the chickpeas. Sprinkle with the remaining fresh cilantro and serve immediately.

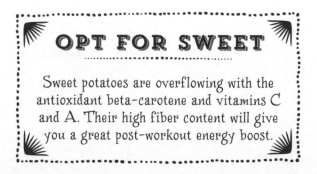

OPT FOR SWEET

Sweet potatoes are overflowing with the antioxidant beta-carotene and vitamins C and A. Their high fiber content will give you a great post-workout energy boost.

CHIPOTLE TURKEY CROQUETTES WITH PARMESAN & FLAXSEED CRUST

It might not look like a healthy snack, but these croquettes are baked instead of fried and the lean turkey is full of healthy minerals.

SERVES: 4　　**PREP: 35–40 MINS**　　**COOK: 20–25 MINS**

1–2 tablespoons olive oil
4 scallions, quartered
1 small red bell pepper, seeded and cut into chunks
1 carrot, coarsely grated
2 teaspoons fresh thyme leaves
1 pound fresh ground turkey breast
1 teaspoon mild paprika
1 small dried chipotle chile, finely chopped
1 egg
1 tablespoon cold water
¼ cup freshly grated Parmesan cheese
⅔ cup flaxseed, finely ground
sea salt and pepper, to taste

AVOCADO DIP
1 large ripe avocado, halved and pitted
grated zest and juice of 1 lime
2 tablespoons fat-free Greek-style yogurt

per serving: 414 cal / 22.4g fat
3.8g sat fat / 14.4g carbs / 3.4g sugars
1.2g salt / 8.9g fiber / 40.3g protein

1. Preheat the oven to 400°F. Brush a baking sheet with a little of the oil. Finely chop the scallions and red bell pepper in a food processor. Add the carrot, thyme, and turkey, then sprinkle with the paprika, chile, and a little salt and pepper. Process until evenly mixed together.

2. Scoop out tablespoons of the mixture onto a cutting board to make 16 oval mounds, then press them into smoother shapes between your hands.

3. Lightly mix together the egg, water, and a little salt and pepper in a shallow dish. Mix the cheese and ground flaxseed in a separate shallow dish. Dip the croquettes, one at a time, into the egg, lift out with two forks, draining well, then roll in the cheese mixture. Place on the prepared baking sheet. Continue until all the croquettes are coated.

4. Bake in the preheated oven for 20–25 minutes, until golden, turning halfway through cooking and brushing with the remaining oil, if needed. To check that they are cooked, cut one croquette in half—the juices should run clear with no traces of pink.

5. When the croquettes are almost ready to serve, make the dip. Scoop the avocado from the shell, mash with the lime zest and juice, and mix with the yogurt. Spoon into a small bowl set on a large plate, then arrange the hot croquettes around the dish and serve immediately.

67

High energy

CHIA SEEDS

Chia seeds were a staple crop among the Mayans and Aztecs, rumored to be more valuable than gold, and for good reason—these tiny seeds are a nutritional powerhouse full of healthy fats and a host of potent antioxidants.

BLUEBERRIES

Blueberries are among the most powerful superfoods, with the same amount of antioxidants as five servings of other fruit and vegetables.

PEANUT BUTTER

Good-quality peanut butter is an excellent source of protein and healthy monounsaturated fats, but be sure to choose organic, unsweetened types so you can maximize the health benefits.

GOJI BERRIES

These little red berries are rich in carotenes, which help to boost the immune system, and some research suggests that regular consumption can protect again heart disease and cancer.

OATS

Oats are a valuable source of whole grains, which help in reducing inflammation and maintaining a healthy weight. They are also high in protein—equal to soy protein—and the hull-free oat kernel (the groat) is the highest of all cereals.

CHICKEN, KALE & CHIA SEED BITES

These bites may be small, but they have an impressive nutritional profile, with lean chicken, leafy kale, and powerful chia seeds.

MAKES: 16　　PREP: 20–25 MINS, PLUS COOLING　　COOK: 21 MINS

2 boneless, skinless chicken breasts (about 4½ ounces)
1 garlic clove, finely chopped
¾ cup shredded kale
½ cup light cream cheese
grated zest of 1 lemon
2 teaspoons chia seeds
sea salt and pepper, to taste

per bite: 36 cal / 1.6g fat
0.7g sat fat / 1.1g carbs / 0.4g sugars
0.3g salt / 0.2g fiber / 4.1g protein

1. Put the chicken breasts into the top of a steamer filled halfway with boiling water. Sprinkle with the garlic, season with salt and pepper, cover with a lid, and cook over medium heat for 20 minutes, or until the juices run clear with no trace of pink when the chicken is pierced with the tip of a sharp knife.

2. Add the kale to the steamer and cook for 1 minute to soften it slightly.

3. Remove the steamer from the pan and let cool, then finely chop the chicken and kale.

4. Mix the cream cheese, lemon zest, and chia seeds together, then stir in the chicken and kale. Taste and adjust the seasoning, if needed.

5. Using two teaspoons, scoop spoonfuls of the mixture onto a plate, scraping it off one spoon with the second spoon. Roll the mixture into balls, then pack into a plastic container. Seal and store in the refrigerator for up to two days.

LOVELY LEFTOVERS

This is a great way to use up leftover roasted chicken. Begin the recipe at step 3 and add the cooked chicken to the cooled kale.

GINGER & OAT NO-BAKE COOKIES

This is a low-sugar version of a granola bar filled with healthy oats.
Sweet and gingery, these cookies have an irresistible flavor.

^^^

MAKES: 8   PREP: 10–15 MINS, PLUS CHILLING   COOK: 8–10 MINS

3½ tablespoons unsalted butter
1 cup heavy cream
1 heaping tablespoon unsweetened smooth peanut butter
3 tablespoons honey
1 tablespoon ground ginger
1⅓ cups steel-cut oats

per cookie: 175 cal / 11.8g fat
6.3g sat fat / 14g carbs / 1.6g sugars
0.2g salt / 2g fiber / 3.8g protein

1. Put the butter, cream, and peanut butter into a saucepan and bring to a boil over medium heat, stirring from time to time. Turn the heat down to medium–low and cook for 5 minutes.

2. Add all the remaining ingredients to the pan and stir to mix well.

3. Line a baking sheet with parchment paper. Drop tablespoons of the dough onto the sheet, then cover and chill in the refrigerator for 25 minutes to harden before serving.

GOJI, MANGO & PISTACHIO POPCORN SLICES

This version of "refrigerator cake" uses mineral-boosting dried fruit and seeds for a nutrient-dense, energy-packed treat.

MAKES: 12   PREP: 25 MINS, PLUS CHILLING   COOK: 6–8 MINS

1 tablespoon light olive oil

3 tablespoons popping corn

½ cup chunky peanut butter

2 tablespoons coconut oil

2 tablespoons maple syrup

⅓ cup whole or low-fat milk

4 ounces bittersweet chocolate, broken into pieces

¼ cup coarsely chopped goji berries

3 tablespoons finely chopped dried mango slices

3 tablespoons coarsely chopped pistachio nuts

1½ tablespoons sunflower seeds

1½ tablespoons pumpkin seeds (pepita)

per slice: 195 cal / 13.8g fat
5.4g sat fat / 13.3g carbs / 7.5g sugars
0.1g salt / 2.2g fiber / 4.5g protein

74

1. Line an 8-inch square, shallow cake pan with a sheet of nonstick parchment paper.

2. Heat the olive oil in a skillet, then add the corn, cover with a lid, and cook over medium heat for 3–4 minutes, until all the corn has popped. Transfer to a bowl, discarding any kernels that haven't popped, and wipe out the pan with paper towels.

3. Add the peanut butter, coconut oil, maple syrup, and milk to the pan and heat gently for 2–3 minutes, stirring until smooth. Remove from the heat, add the chocolate, and set aside for 4–5 minutes, until the chocolate has melted.

4. Add the popcorn to the chocolate mix and lightly stir together. Transfer to the prepared cake pan, press down flat with the back of a fork, then sprinkle with the goji berries, mango, pistachios, sunflower seeds, and pumpkin seeds. Press the topping into the soft chocolate mix, then chill in the refrigerator for 2 hours, until firmly set.

5. Lift the chocolate mixture out of the pan, place on a cutting board, peel away and reserve the paper, then cut the slice into 12 pieces. Pack into a plastic container, layering with the reserved paper. Keep in the refrigerator for up to four days.

CHOCOLATE & PEANUT BUTTER ENERGY BALLS

Bittersweet chocolate contains the same powerful antioxidant found in red wine and can help a variety of health conditions.

MAKES: 8   PREP: 20–25 MINS, PLUS CHILLING   COOK: NO COOKING

½ cup blanched almonds

¼ cup unsweetened peanut butter

2 tablespoons coarsely chopped unsalted peanuts

3 tablespoons flaxseed

1 ounce bittersweet chocolate, finely chopped

1 teaspoon unsweetened cocoa powder

sea salt

per ball: 144 cal / 11.9g fat
2.1g sat fat / 5.9g carbs / 1.7g sugars
0.3g salt / 3g fiber / 4.9g protein

1. Put the almonds into a food processor and process for a minute, until you have the texture of coarse flour.

2. Put the peanut butter, peanuts, flaxseed, chocolate, and a small pinch of salt into a bowl and mix. Add the almond flour, reserving 1½ tablespoons. Mix until you have a texture resembling chunky clay.

3. Sprinkle the remaining almond flour and the cocoa powder onto a plate and mix with a teaspoon. Form a tablespoon-size blob of the peanut mixture into a ball, using the palms of your hands. Roll it in the cocoa powder mixture, then transfer to a plate. Make another seven balls in the same way.

4. Cover and chill in the refrigerator for at least 30 minutes before serving. Serve or store in the refrigerator for up to two days.

BANANA FLATBREAD BITES WITH TAHINI & DATE SYRUP

Sometimes the best things are the simplest. Assembled in minutes, this snack is perfect for combating the midafternoon energy slump.

SERVES: 4   PREP: 15–20 MINS   COOK: 5–6 MINS

4 (8-inch) whole-wheat tortillas
¼ cup tahini
3 tablespoons date syrup
4 bananas, peeled

per serving: 354 cal / 11.3g fat
2.5g sat fat / 60g carbs / 25.4g sugars
0.5g salt / 4.1g fiber / 9.4g protein

1. Preheat a dry skillet, then add the tortillas, one by one, and warm for 30 seconds on each side.

2. Arrange the tortillas on a cutting board, thinly spread each with the tahini, then drizzle with the date syrup. Add a whole banana to each tortilla, just a little off-center, then roll up tightly.

3. Cut each tortilla into thick slices, secure the bites with a toothpick, and arrange on a plate. Serve warm.

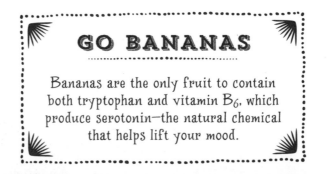

GO BANANAS

Bananas are the only fruit to contain both tryptophan and vitamin B_6, which produce serotonin—the natural chemical that helps lift your mood.

4

WEEKEND SNACKS

Weekend snacks are inevitable, but even these
need not be processed and unhealthy with this
collection of tasty recipes—ideal for when you
have just a little extra time to prepare.

CHICKEN SATAY SKEWERS WITH PEANUT SAUCE

Chicken is one of the best sources of lean protein, and peanut butter contains loads of healthy monounsaturated fats.

SERVES: 4   PREP: 25–30 MINS, PLUS MARINATING   COOK: 6–8 MINS

4 boneless, skinless chicken breasts (about 4 ounces each), cut into ¾-inch cubes
¼ cup soy sauce
1 tablespoon cornstarch
2 garlic cloves, finely chopped
1-inch piece fresh ginger, peeled and finely chopped
1 cucumber, diced, to serve

PEANUT SAUCE
2 tablespoons peanut or vegetable oil
½ onion, finely chopped
1 garlic clove, finely chopped
¼ cup chunky peanut butter
¼–⅓ cup water
½ teaspoon chili powder

per serving: 327 cal / 16.8g fat
2.9g sat fat / 12.6g carbs / 3.7g sugars
2.4g salt / 2.2g fiber / 32.4g protein

1. Put the chicken cubes into a shallow dish. Mix together the soy sauce, cornstarch, garlic, and ginger in a small bowl and pour the marinade over the chicken. Cover and let marinate in the refrigerator for at least 2 hours.

2. Meanwhile, soak 12 wooden skewers in cold water for at least 30 minutes. Preheat the broiler to medium–high and thread the chicken pieces onto the wooden skewers. Transfer the skewers to a broiler pan and cook under the preheated broiler for 3–4 minutes. Turn the skewers over and cook for an additional 3–4 minutes, or until cooked all the way through. To make sure the chicken is cooked, cut into the middle to check there are no remaining traces of pink or red.

3. Meanwhile, to make the sauce, heat the oil in a saucepan, add the onion and garlic, and cook over medium heat, stirring frequently, for 3–4 minutes, until softened. Add the peanut butter, water, and chili powder and simmer for 2–3 minutes, until softened and thinned. Serve the skewers immediately with the warm sauce and cucumber.

KALE & GREEN GARLIC BRUSCHETTA

Green or "wet" garlic is the garlic from the first crop of the season.
Soft and delicious, it is excellent spread on toast.

SERVES: 4   **PREP: 25 MINS**   **COOK: 25 MINS**

1 green garlic bulb
3 tablespoons olive oil
4 slices sourdough bread or multigrain bread
1 cup shredded kale
1 tablespoon balsamic vinegar
2 teaspoons pomegranate molasses
sea salt and pepper, to taste

per serving: 278 cal / 1.3g fat
1.7g sat fat / 35.4g carbs / 3.6g sugars
1.4g salt / 4.8g fiber / 7.3g protein

1. Preheat the oven to 375°F. Put the garlic bulb onto a piece of aluminum foil, drizzle with 1 tablespoon of the oil, then wrap the foil around it and seal well. Put onto a baking sheet and roast in the preheated oven for 20 minutes, or until the bulb feels soft when squeezed.

2. Meanwhile, preheat a ridged grill pan. Cut the bread slices in half, brush one side of each with a little oil, then cook the bread, oiled-side down, in the hot pan for 2 minutes. Brush the top with the remaining oil, then turn and cook the second side until golden brown.

3. Unwrap the garlic, peel away the outer casing from the bulb, separate the cloves, then remove any of the tougher skins. Crush the creamy, soft garlic to a coarse paste, using a mortar and pestle. Mix the paste with any juices from the foil, then thinly spread on the grilled bread and keep warm.

4. Heat a dry, nonstick skillet, add the kale, and cook over medium heat for 2–3 minutes, until just wilted. Mix in the vinegar, molasses, and a little salt and pepper. Arrange the bruschetta on a cutting board, spoon the kale over it, and serve.

GO GREEN

Green, leafy vegetables, such as kale, Swiss chard, and cabbage, are rich in iron and contain the pigment chlorophyll, which helps to increase the oxygenation of the blood.

CHICKEN-AND CHEESE-STUFFED MINI BELL PEPPERS

Filled with oozing cheese, these tasty little mouthfuls are perfect for serving as appetizers at a dinner party.

MAKES: 12   PREP: 30–35 MINS   COOK: 15 MINS

olive oil, for oiling
⅓ cup cream cheese
2 garlic cloves, finely chopped
2 teaspoons finely chopped fresh rosemary
1 tablespoon finely chopped fresh basil
1 tablespoon finely chopped fresh flat-leaf parsley
3 tablespoons finely grated Parmesan cheese
1 cup finely chopped cooked chicken breast
3 scallions, finely chopped
12 mixed colored baby bell peppers (about 12 ounces)
sea salt and pepper, to taste

per stuffed bell pepper: 59 cal / 3.2g fat
1.5g sat fat / 2.4g carbs / 1.7g sugars
0.4g salt / 0.7g fiber / 5g protein

1. Preheat the oven to 375°F. Lightly brush a large baking sheet with oil.

2. Put the cream cheese, garlic, rosemary, basil, and parsley into a bowl, then add the Parmesan and stir together with a metal spoon.

3. Mix in the chicken and scallions, then season with a little salt and pepper.

4. Slice each bell pepper from the bottom up to the stem, leaving the stem in place, then make a small cut just to the side, so that you can get a teaspoon into the center of the pepper to scoop out the seeds.

5. Fill each bell pepper with some of the chicken mixture, then place on the prepared baking sheet. Cook in the preheated oven for 15 minutes, or until the bell peppers are soft and light brown in patches.

6. Let cool slightly on the baking sheet, then transfer to a serving plate. Serve warm or cold. These are best eaten on the day they are made and should be kept in the refrigerator if serving cold.

FLAVOR TWIST

For a spicy, smoky twist, try adding ½ teaspoon crushed red pepper flakes and ½ teaspoon smoked paprika to the cheese mixture before stuffing the bell peppers.

FAVA BEAN & MINT HUMMUS WITH CRUDITES

This summery hummus, made with freshly shelled fava beans and flavored with chopped herbs, is delicious with warm pita breads.

SERVES: 4 **PREP: 30–35 MINS** **COOK: 15 MINS**

2 cups shelled fava beans
2 tablespoons virgin olive oil
1 teaspoon cumin seeds, crushed
3 scallions, thinly sliced
2 garlic cloves, finely chopped
½ cup torn fresh mint pieces
¼ cup finely chopped fresh flat-leaf parsley
juice of 1 lemon
⅓ cup Greek-style plain yogurt
sea salt and pepper, to taste

TO SERVE

1 red and 1 yellow bell pepper, seeded and cut into strips
4 celery stalks, cut into strips
½ cucumber, halved, seeded and cut into strips
pita breads, warmed and cut into strips (optional)

per serving: 446 cal / 13.7g fat
2.5g sat fat / 67.7g carbs / 8.4g sugars
2.3g salt / 15.5g fiber / 19.1g protein

1. Fill the bottom of a steamer halfway with water, bring to a boil, then put the fava beans in the top of the steamer, cover with a lid, and steam for 10 minutes, or until tender.

2. Meanwhile, heat the oil in a skillet over medium heat. Add the cumin, scallions, and garlic, and cook for 2 minutes, or until the scallions are softened.

3. Put the beans in a food processor or blender, add the onion mixture, herbs, lemon juice, and yogurt and season with a little salt and pepper. Process to a coarse puree, then spoon into a dish set on a large plate.

4. Arrange the vegetable strips around the hummus and serve with the pita breads, if using.

VIETNAMESE SHRIMP SPRING ROLLS

Wonderfully light, gluten-free, and practically fat-free, these snacks are full of protein-rich shellfish and crunchy raw vegetables.

MAKES: 6   **PREP: 40 MINS**   **COOK: NO COOKING**

1½ ounces vermicelli rice noodles

5½ ounces cooked and chilled jumbo shrimp, rinsed with cold water, drained, and thickly sliced

grated zest of 1 lime

¼ cup torn fresh mint

6 sprigs fresh cilantro, long stems trimmed

½ cup bean sprouts

1 carrot, cut into matchstick strips

¼ cucumber, halved lengthwise, seeded, and cut into matchstick strips

½ romaine lettuce heart, leaves shredded

6 (8-inch) rice spring roll wrappers

DIPPING SAUCE

juice of 1 lime

1 tablespoon tamari

1 tablespoon packed light brown sugar

1 teaspoon Thai fish sauce

1 red chile, halved, seeded, and finely chopped

2 garlic cloves, finely chopped

1-inch piece fresh ginger, scrubbed and finely grated

per roll: 112 cal / 0.4g fat
trace sat fat / 22.2g carbs / 4.3g sugars
1.3g salt / 1.6g fiber / 5g protein

1. Add the noodles to a shallow dish, cover with just-boiled water, then let soften for 5 minutes, or prepare according to the package directions.

2. Mix the shrimp with the lime zest. Arrange the mint, cilantro, bean sprouts, carrot sticks, cucumber sticks, and shredded lettuce in separate piles on a tray. Drain the noodles and put into a dish.

3. Pour some just-boiled water into a large, shallow dish, then dip one of the rice wrappers into the water. Keep moving it in the water for 10–15 seconds, until soft and transparent, then lift out, drain well, and place on a cutting board.

4. Arrange a few shrimp in a horizontal line in the center of the rice wrapper, leaving a border of wrapper at either end. Top with some mint leaves and a cilantro sprig, then add a few noodles and bean sprouts. Add some carrot and cucumber, and a little lettuce. Roll up the bottom third of the rice wrapper over the filling, fold in the sides, then roll up tightly to form a log shape. Place on a plate.

5. Repeat with the remaining wrappers until you have 12 rolls.

6. To make the dip, add the lime juice to a small bowl, stir in the tamari, sugar, and Thai fish sauce, then add the chopped chile, garlic, and ginger, and stir.

7. Cut each roll in half and serve immediately with individual bowls of the dipping sauce. If planning to serve later, wrap each roll in plastic wrap and chill in the refrigerator for up to 8 hours.

Weekend snacks

MINT

Mint has soothing, anesthetic properties and is effective at calming the stomach. Mint tea made simply by steeping the fresh leaves in boiling water is also a good cure for hiccups.

CHILES

Hot chiles do more than add a little spice to your meals—their heat is also great for boosting the metabolism by increasing body temperature, which can help with weight loss.

PECANS

Pecans are packed with plant sterols, which are effective at lowering cholesterol. They also contain high levels of oleic acid, the healthy fat found in avocados and olives.

ALMOND MILK

More than being a substitute for dairy milk, almond and other nut milks are great for getting a little extra protein into your diet. Try to buy organic where possible, because it uses real almonds for sweetness instead of added sugar.

FIGS

Originating in Asia, figs have an illustrious history. They are high in natural sugars, which, like dates, make them perfect for adding a healthier dose of sweetness to any dish.

BAKED FIGS WITH GORGONZOLA

Made with baby figs, just-melting Gorgonzola, delicate wildflower honey, and crunchy multigrain toast, this snack is heavenly.

SERVES: 4 PREP: 15 MINS COOK: 10 MINS

1 small multigrain baguette, cut into eight ¾-inch-thick slices

8 small fresh figs

2 ounces Gorgonzola cheese or other blue cheese, rind removed, cut into 8 squares

4 teaspoons wildflower honey

per serving: 195 cal / 5.2g fat 2.8g sat fat / 28g carbs / 16.1g sugars 0.7g salt / 4.2g fiber / 6.9g protein

94

1. Preheat the oven to 350°F. Lightly toast the bread on both sides, then transfer to a small baking sheet.

2. Cut a cross in the top of each fig, lightly press a cube of cheese into each one, then place a fig on top of each slice of toast. Bake in the preheated oven for 5–6 minutes, until the figs are hot and the cheese is just melting.

3. Transfer to a plate or cutting board. Drizzle with honey and serve immediately.

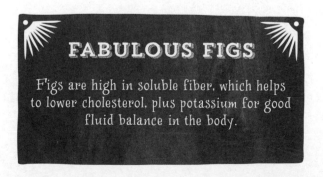

FABULOUS FIGS

Figs are high in soluble fiber, which helps to lower cholesterol, plus potassium for good fluid balance in the body.

APPLE & CINNAMON CHIPS

Crisp and crunchy, without the fat and strong flavors of potato chips, these make a much healthier alternative for all the family.

SERVES: 4   PREP: 20–25 MINS, PLUS COOLING   COOK: 1½–2 HRS

4 cups water
1 tablespoon sea salt
3 crisp, sweet apples
pinch of ground cinnamon

per serving: 72 cal / 0.2g fat
trace sat fat / 19.1g carbs / 14.2g sugars
0.7g salt / 3.4g fiber / 0.3g protein

96

1. Preheat the oven to 225°F. Put the water and salt into a large mixing bowl and stir until the salt has dissolved.

2. Thinly slice the apples, one at a time, with a sharp knife or mandoline, leaving the skin on and the core still in place, but removing any seeds. Add each apple slice to the water. Turn to coat in the salt water, which will help prevent discoloration.

3. Drain the apple slices in a colander, then lightly pat dry with a clean dish towel. Arrange in a thin layer on a large roasting rack. Place it in the oven so that the heat can circulate under the slices as well as over the tops.

4. Bake for 1½–2 hours, until the apple slices are dry and crisp. Loosen with a spatula and transfer to a large plate or cutting board, then sprinkle with cinnamon. Let cool completely, then serve or pack into a plastic container, seal, and keep in the refrigerator for up to two days.

HOMEMADE CACAO & HAZELNUT BUTTER

This delicious nut butter, made with wholesome ingredients, is perfect spread on whole-grain toast or hot pancakes for a weekend treat.

MAKES: ABOUT 3/4 CUP   PREP: 15 MINS, PLUS STANDING   COOK: 3–4 MINS

1 cup unblanched hazelnuts
⅓ cup raw cacao powder
¼ cup firmly packed light brown sugar
½ cup light olive oil
½ teaspoon natural vanilla extract
pinch of sea salt
whole-grain toast or pancakes, to serve (optional)

per 3 tablespoon serving: 430 cal
40g fat / 5.2g sat fat / 19.5g carbs
13.9g sugars 0.3g salt / 4g fiber
4.1g protein

1. Add the hazelnuts to a dry skillet and cook over medium heat for 3–4 minutes, constantly shaking the pan, until the nuts are an even golden brown.

2. Wrap the nuts in a clean dish towel and rub to remove the skins.

3. Put the nuts into a food processor or blender and process until finely ground. Add the cacao powder, sugar, oil, vanilla extract, and salt, and process again to make a smooth paste. Spoon into a small jar, seal tightly, and let stand at room temperature for 4 hours, until the sugar has dissolved completely. Stir again, then store in the refrigerator for up to five days. Serve on whole-grain toast or hot pancakes, if using.

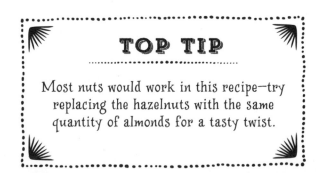

TOP TIP

Most nuts would work in this recipe—try replacing the hazelnuts with the same quantity of almonds for a tasty twist.

SQUASH & PECAN PANCAKES

Pancakes are the ultimate weekend treat and the addition of nuts and nutrient-rich squash in this recipe gives them a healthy boost.

SERVES: 6　　PREP: 20 MINS　　COOK: 25–30 MINS

1 cup plus 2 tablespoons all-purpose flour

3 tablespoons chopped pecans

¼ cup firmly packed light brown sugar

2 teaspoons baking powder

½ teaspoon cinnamon

¼ teaspoon sea salt

1 egg

1¼ cups low-fat buttermilk

¾ cup mashed, cooked butternut squash or other squash

1 teaspoon natural vanilla extract

vegetable oil spray

½ cup honey or maple syrup, to serve (optional)

per serving: 246 cal / 4.6g fat
1.1g sat fat / 45.2g carbs / 24.2g sugars
1.5g salt / 1.4g fiber / 6.1g protein

1. In a medium bowl, combine the flour with the pecans, sugar, baking powder, cinnamon, and salt. In another large bowl, whisk together the egg, buttermilk, squash, and vanilla extract. Whisk the dry ingredients into the wet ingredients and mix well.

2. Spray a nonstick skillet with the vegetable oil spray and heat over medium–high heat. When hot, ladle in the batter, ¼ cup at a time, to make 3–4-inch pancakes.

3. Cook for 2–3 minutes, or until bubbles begin to form on the surface and the bottom is lightly browned. Flip over and cook for an additional 2 minutes, or until the second side is lightly browned. Serve immediately with honey, if using.

101

ALMOND MILK-AND-COOKIE SHOTS

Refreshing almond milk served in a chocolate-lined, whole-grain hazelnut cookie—who said eating healthily was dull?

MAKES: 6   PREP: 35 MINS, PLUS CHILLING   COOK: 18–20 MINS

⅓ cup coconut oil, at room temperature, plus extra for oiling

¼ cup firmly packed light brown sugar

½ teaspoon natural vanilla extract

¼ cup ground hazelnuts

2 tablespoons flaxseed, ground

1 cup whole-wheat flour

1 egg yolk

4 ounces bittersweet chocolate

⅔ cup unsweetened almond milk

per shot: 573 cal / 39.7g fat
24.8g sat fat / 50.2g carbs / 21.4g sugars
trace salt / 8.2g fiber / 8.6g protein

1. Lightly grease six ⅓-cup dariole molds and line each bottom with a circle of parchment paper.

2. Beat together the coconut oil, sugar, and vanilla extract in a mixing bowl or food processor until light and creamy. Add the hazelnuts and flaxseeds, then add the flour and egg yolk and beat together. Finely chop 1 ounce of the chocolate and mix into the cookie crumbs. Using your hands, squeeze the dough into crumbly clumps.

3. Divide the dough among the prepared molds, then level with the back of a teaspoon. Transfer to a baking pan and chill in the refrigerator for 20 minutes. Meanwhile, preheat the oven to 350°F.

4. Bake in the preheated oven for 13–15 minutes, until golden brown, then reshape the inside of the cups with the back of a small teaspoon. Let cool for 30 minutes.

5. Loosen the edges of the cups with a small, blunt knife and remove from the molds. Return to the baking pan and chill for at least 1 hour, until firmly set.

6. Chop the remaining chocolate and put into a heatproof bowl set over a saucepan of gently simmering water and heat until melted. Add spoonfuls of melted chocolate to the cookie cups, tilting to evenly cover the insides with chocolate. Chill for at least 30 minutes. When ready to serve, pour in the almond milk and serve on small saucers.

5

SWEET INDULGENCE

The best part about eating healthy, whole foods is that even desserts aren't off-limits if you're doing it right. This chapter contains plenty of ideas for healthier sweet snacks for when the cravings kick in.

CHOCOLATE & MACADAMIA 'CUPCAKES'

These delicious mouthfuls are a hybrid between a cupcake and a cookie, and make a nutty and delicious wholesome treat.

MAKES: 12   PREP: 30 MINS, PLUS COOLING   COOK: 20 MINS

6 tablespoons butter, at room temperature

⅓ cup chunky peanut butter

⅓ cup firmly packed light brown sugar

2 eggs, beaten

1 cup whole wheat flour

1 teaspoon baking powder

⅓ cup coarsely chopped macadamia nuts, plus 12 whole nuts to decorate (optional)

CHOCOLATE FROSTING

4 ounces bittersweet chocolate, chopped

2 tablespoons butter, diced

2 tablespoons packed light brown sugar

¼ cup milk

per cupcake: 274 cal / 19.2g fat 8.3g sat fat / 22.3g carbs / 12.3g sugars 0.5g salt / 2.9g fiber / 5.4g protein

1. Preheat the oven to 350°F. Line a 12-cup muffin pan with muffin cups.

2. Put the butter, peanut butter, and sugar into a large bowl or food processor and beat together until light and fluffy.

3. Gradually beat a little of the egg into the butter mixture, alternating with a few spoonfuls of the flour, then continue until all the egg and flour have been added and the batter is smooth. Beat in the baking powder and chopped nuts.

4. Divide the batter among the muffin cups, bake in the preheated oven for 15 minutes, until risen, golden brown, and the tops spring back when lightly pressed with a fingertip. Let cool in the pan for 10 minutes.

5. To make the frosting, put the chocolate, butter, sugar, and milk into a heatproof bowl set over a saucepan of gently simmering water and heat, stirring occasionally, for about 5 minutes, until smooth.

6. Spoon the frosting over the cakes to cover them completely, then top each with a macadamia nut, if using. Let stand in a cool place for 30 minutes to cool completely. Remove from the pan and serve, or store any leftovers in a plastic container in the refrigerator for up to one day.

STRAWBERRY & PASSION FRUIT YOGURTS

If you want a light, sweet-tasting snack, these little jars full of summery freshness will give you an instant boost.

SERVES: 4   **PREP: 20–25 MINS, PLUS COOLING**   **COOK: 2–3 MINS**

¼ cup dried coconut flakes

8 ounces strawberries, hulled

finely grated zest and juice of 1 lime

1½ cups fat-free Greek-style yogurt

4 teaspoons honey

2 passion fruit, halved

1 tablespoon coarsely chopped dried goji berries

per serving: 141 cal / 3.5g fat
2.8g sat fat / 19.3g carbs / 14.6g sugars
trace salt / 3.2g fiber / 10.4g protein

1. Add the coconut to a dry skillet and cook over medium heat for 2–3 minutes, shaking the pan, until light golden. Remove from the heat and let cool.

2. Coarsely mash the strawberries and mix with half the lime juice.

3. Add the lime zest, remaining lime juice, the yogurt, and honey to a bowl, and stir together. Add three-quarters of the cooled coconut to the yogurt, then scoop the seeds from the passion fruit over the top and lightly fold into the yogurt.

4. Layer alternate spoonfuls of strawberry and yogurt in four 8-ounce jars, then sprinkle with the remaining coconut and the goji berries. Tightly seal the jars and chill until ready to serve. Eat within 24 hours.

RUBY FRUIT JUICE

There's nothing more refreshing than locally grown strawberries in the summer, but this smoothie can be enjoyed at any time of year.

SERVES: 1   PREP: 15 MINS   COOK: NO COOKING

1 ruby grapefruit, zest and a little pith removed, seeded and coarsely chopped
¼ cucumber, coarsely chopped
1 cup hulled strawberries
small handful of crushed ice (optional)

1. Put the grapefruit and cucumber into a blender and blend until smooth.

2. Add the strawberries and crushed ice, if using, and blend again until combined.

3. Pour into a glass and serve immediately.

110

per serving: 162 cal / 0.8g fat
trace sat fat / 40.4g carbs / 25.5g sugars
trace salt / 7.3g fiber / 3.4g protein

BLACK BEAN BROWNIES

Don't let on that these gluten-free brownies are made with black beans and dates until everyone is begging for seconds.

MAKES: 16 PREP: 25 MINS, PLUS COOLING COOK: 28 MINS

½ cup bittersweet chocolate chips
3 tablespoons coconut oil
1 (15-ounce) can black beans in water, drained
7 medjool dates, halved and pitted
3 eggs
⅓ cup firmly packed light brown sugar
1 teaspoon natural vanilla extract
⅔ cup unsweetened cocoa powder
1½ teaspoons baking powder
½ teaspoon ground cinnamon
¼ teaspoon sea salt

per brownie: 139 cal / 6.8g fat
4.4g sat fat / 17.6g carbs / 12.3g sugars
0.4g salt / 4g fiber / 3.7g protein

1. Preheat the oven to 350°F. Line an 8-inch square, shallow cake pan with nonstick parchment paper.

2. Add ⅓ cup of the chocolate chips to a small saucepan with the oil and heat over low heat until the oil has melted, then remove and let stand for a few minutes, until the chocolate has melted completely.

3. Meanwhile, add the beans and dates to a food processor or blender and process to a coarse puree. Add the eggs, sugar, vanilla extract, chocolate-and-coconut oil mixture, and process again until smooth.

4. Mix the cocoa powder, baking powder, cinnamon, and salt together, then add to the bean mixture and process briefly until smooth.

5. Spoon into the prepared pan and spread in an even layer. Bake in the preheated oven for about 25 minutes, or until the cake is well risen, beginning to crack around the edges, and still slightly soft in the center.

6. Sprinkle with the remaining chocolate chips and let cool for 20 minutes. Lift the paper and brownies out of the pan and transfer to a wire rack to cool completely. Cut into 16 small pieces, lift off the paper, and store in an airtight container for up to two days.

113

COCONUT MILK, STRAWBERRY & HONEY ICE CREAM

Everyone loves ice cream, but it can be loaded with sugar.
This version is made with just three wholesome ingredients.

SERVES: 6   PREP: 30 MINS, PLUS FREEZING   COOK: NO COOKING

1 pound strawberries,
hulled and halved

1¾ cups coconut milk

⅓ cup honey

crushed hazelnuts, to serve
(optional)

per serving: 198 cal / 14.4g fat
12.6g sat fat / 19.3g carbs / 16.7g sugars
trace salt / 1.8g fiber / 1.4g protein

114

1. Puree the strawberries in a food processor or blender, then press through a strainer set over a mixing bowl to remove the seeds.

2. Add the coconut milk and honey to the strawberry puree and whisk together.

3. Pour the mixture into a large roasting pan to a depth of ¾ inch, cover the top of the pan with plastic wrap, then freeze for about 2 hours, until just set.

4. Scoop back into the food processor or blender and process again until smooth to break down the ice crystals. Pour into a plastic container or 9 x 5-inch loaf pan lined with nonstick parchment paper. Place the lid on the plastic container or fold the paper over the ice cream in the loaf pan. Return to the freezer for 3–4 hours, or until firm enough to scoop.

5. Serve immediately or store in the freezer until needed. Thaw at room temperature for 15 minutes to soften slightly, then scoop into individual dishes and top with crushed hazelnuts, if using, to serve.

Sweet indulgence

STRAWBERRIES

Strawberries have been popular since the Roman times and are native to many parts of the world. Like many other fruits, strawberries were historically considered a luxury item only enjoyed by royalty.

PINK GRAPEFRUIT

Grapefruit has long been hailed as a diet food because of its nutritional profile, being low in calories and high in phytonutrients. It's loaded with vitamin C, too, with just half a grapefruit meeting 78 percent of your daily vitamin C requirement.

PASSION FRUIT

As well as adding a sweet tang to a dessert, passion fruit pulp is also a good source of potassium, making it useful for lowering blood pressure.

COCONUT

Coconut boasts an array of health benefits, mostly due to its high levels of lauric acid, an antifungal, antiviral "miracle" ingredient, which is great for boosting the immune system.

CHOCOLATE

Bittersweet chocolate and, particularly, raw cacao, has been shown to have many health benefits, including protecting the nervous system. Choose chocolate with 70 percent cocoa solids or higher, such as bittersweet chocolate, to be sure of a minimal sugar content.

SUPERFOOD CHOCOLATE BARK

The darker the chocolate, the less sugar and more cocoa butter it contains, so always choose bittersweet chocolate.

SERVES: 6   **PREP: 20 MINS, PLUS SETTING**   **COOK: 5 MINS**

4 ounces bittersweet chocolate, chopped

¾ cup coarsely chopped mixed Brazil nuts, unblanched almonds, and pistachio nuts

2 tablespoons coarsely chopped dried goji berries

2 tablespoons coarsely chopped dried cranberries

1 tablespoon chia seeds

per serving: 227 cal / 15.7g fat
5.3g sat fat / 17.7g carbs / 10.2g sugars
trace salt / 5.1g fiber / 5.1g protein

1. Put the chocolate into a heatproof bowl set over a saucepan of gently simmering water and heat for 5 minutes, until melted, making sure that the bottom of the bowl is not touching the water.

2. Line a large baking sheet with nonstick parchment paper. Stir the chocolate, then pour it onto the paper and spread into an 8 x 12-inch rectangle.

3. Sprinkle the nuts, berries, and chia seeds over the top, then let set in a cool place or the refrigerator.

4. To serve, lift the chocolate off the paper and break into shards. Store in a plastic container in the refrigerator for up to three days.

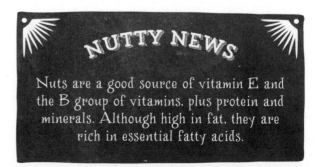

NUTTY NEWS

Nuts are a good source of vitamin E and the B group of vitamins, plus protein and minerals. Although high in fat, they are rich in essential fatty acids.

MINI ROASTED PEACH & RASPBERRY BLINIS

These dainty Russian pancakes make the perfect light treat. In the time it takes to make them, the roasted fruit topping will be ready.

MAKES: 20 **PREP: 30 MINS** **COOK: 30–40 MINS**

4 small peaches, halved, pitted, and cut into chunks
1 tablespoon maple syrup
2 tablespoons water
1¼ cups raspberries
⅔ cup crème fraîche or sour cream
1 teaspoon natural vanilla extract

BLINI BATTER
¾ cup buckwheat flour
1 teaspoon baking powder
1 egg
½ cup low-fat milk
1 tablespoon light olive oil, for frying
sea salt

per blini: 59 cal / 2.7g fat
1.1g sat fat / 7.6g carbs / 3.8g sugars
0.3g salt / 1.3g fiber / 1.6g protein

1. Preheat the oven to 375°F. Put the peaches into a small roasting pan, drizzle with the maple syrup and water, then roast in the preheated oven for 10 minutes, until soft and just beginning to brown around the edges. Remove from the oven, sprinkle the raspberries into the hot pan, and set aside.

2. Mix the crème fraîche or sour cream with the vanilla extract and set aside.

3. To make the blinis, put the flour, baking powder, and a pinch of salt into a bowl and stir together. Add the egg, then gradually whisk in the milk until smooth.

4. Heat the oil in a large skillet and pour out any excess into a small bowl. Drop tablespoons of the batter over the bottom of the pan, leaving a little space between each. Cook over medium heat for 2–3 minutes, until bubbles begin to show on the surface and the undersides are golden brown. Turn over with a spatula and cook for an additional 1–2 minutes.

5. Lift the blinis out of the pan with a spatula and keep warm in a clean dish towel. Heat the reserved oil in the pan, pour out the excess, then continue cooking the blinis, in batches, until all the batter has been used.

6. Layer the blinis on a large plate with the crème fraîche and warm fruit, and serve immediately.

CHOCOLATE & AVOCADO PUDDINGS

Unlike traditional chocolate mousses, this version doesn't need to be chilled and can be served just minutes after making.

MAKES: 4   PREP: 20 MINS   COOK: 5 MINS

2 ounces bittersweet chocolate, chopped
1 large ripe avocado, halved and pitted
¼ cup coconut milk
4 teaspoons maple syrup
½ teaspoon natural vanilla extract
pinch of sea salt
grated bitterwsweet chocolate and lightly toasted coconut chips, to decorate (optional)

per pudding: 246 cal / 16.4g fat
7.3g sat fat / 24.5g carbs / 16.1g sugars
0.4g salt / 4.9g fiber / 2.4g protein

1. Put the chocolate into a heatproof bowl set over a saucepan of gently simmering water and heat for 5 minutes, making sure that the water doesn't touch the bottom of the bowl.

2. Scoop the avocado flesh from the skin into a food processor. Process until smooth, then add the coconut milk, maple syrup, vanilla extract, and salt. Spoon in the melted chocolate and process until smooth.

3. Spoon the mixture into small shot glasses. Decorate the tops with a little grated chocolate and a few toasted coconut chips, if using. Serve immediately or chill in the refrigerator until needed.

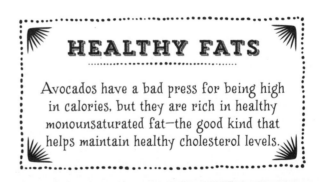

HEALTHY FATS

Avocados have a bad press for being high in calories, but they are rich in healthy monounsaturated fat—the good kind that helps maintain healthy cholesterol levels.

RHUBARB & LEMON DRIZZLE SQUARES

Sometimes you just need a piece of cake—this healthier brown rice flour and almond cake is perfect for a midafternoon pick-me-up.

MAKES: 9   PREP: 30–35 MINS, PLUS COOLING   COOK: 35–40 MINS

6 trimmed young rhubarb stalks, cut into ¾-inch thick slices
1 cup ground almonds
1 cup brown rice flour
1½ teaspoons baking powder
1 ripe banana, mashed
⅔ cup rice bran oil
½ cup firmly packed light brown sugar
grated zest of 1 lemon
3 eggs
¼ cup coarsely chopped unblanched almonds

SYRUP
juice of 2 lemons
¼ cup firmly packed light brown sugar

per square: 400 cal / 26.1g fat
4.5g sat fat / 37.7g carbs / 22.6g sugars
0.6g salt / 3.2g fiber / 6.8g protein

1. Preheat the oven to 350°F. Line a 12 x 8 x 1½-inch cake pan with nonstick parchment paper.

2. Put the rhubarb into a dry roasting pan and bake in the preheated oven for 10 minutes, until almost soft. Remove from the oven but do not turn off the oven.

3. Put the ground almonds, flour, and baking powder into a bowl and stir together.

4. Put the banana, oil, sugar, and lemon zest into a separate bowl and whisk together until smooth. Whisk in the eggs, one at a time, then beat in the flour mixture.

5. Spoon the batter into the prepared pan, then sprinkle the rhubarb over the top. Bake in the preheated oven for 25–30 minutes, until the cake is well risen and the sponge springs back when pressed with a fingertip.

6. To make the syrup, mix the lemon juice with the sugar. Spoon half over the hot cake and let soak in for 1–2 minutes. Spoon over the remaining syrup, sprinkle with the chopped almonds, and let cool in the pan.

7. Lift the cake out of the pan, peel away the paper, and cut into 9 pieces. Eat within two days or freeze until needed.

FROZEN YOGURT-COATED BERRIES

These look like candies but they are bursting with fruity freshness, vitamin C, and calcium. Keep a handy supply in the freezer.

SERVES: 4   PREP: 20–25 MINS, PLUS FREEZING   COOK: NO COOKING

1 cup fat-free Greek-style yogurt
1 tablespoon honey
¼ teaspoon natural vanilla extract
¾ cup blueberries
1 cup raspberries

per serving: 81 cal / 0.3g fat
trace sat fat / 14.5g carbs / 10.8g sugars
trace salt / 2.7g fiber / 6.4g protein

1. Line three baking sheets that will fit in your freezer with nonstick parchment paper.

2. Put the yogurt, honey, and vanilla extract into a medium bowl and stir together. Drop a few blueberries into the yogurt, then use two forks to coat the berries in a thin layer of yogurt. Lift out, one berry at a time, draining off the excess yogurt, and transfer to one of the lined sheets.

3. Continue dipping and coating until all the blueberries are on the baking sheet. Repeat with the raspberries. Freeze, uncovered, for 2–3 hours, until frozen hard.

4. Lift the berries from the baking sheets and pack into plastic bags or lidded plastic containers. Seal and freeze for up to one month.

5. Remove as many as you need from the freezer and let thaw for 10 minutes before serving so that the fruit can soften slightly.

INDEX